KEEP

JOHN TRACY **5**   GORDON TRACY **4**   ALAN TRACY **3**   VIRGIL TRACY **2**   SCOTT TRACY **1**

This edition published by Parragon Books Ltd in 2015

Parragon Books Ltd
Chartist House
15–17 Trim Street
Bath BA1 1HA, UK
www.parragon.com

STUDIOS

ISBN 978-1-4748-0116-4

Printed in Poland

THUNDERBIRDS ARE GO

ANNUAL 2016

THUNDERBiRDS

ARE GO

INSIDE

07 INTERNATIONAL RESCUE TEAM
08 PERSONNEL PROFILE: SCOTT TRACY
10 VEHICLE DOSSIER: THUNDERBIRD 1
12 PUZZLE: MISSION LOG
14 ACTIVITY: BUILD THUNDERBIRD 1
18 PUZZLE: CODE CONFUSION
19 PUZZLE: FAST RESPONSE
20 SECRET REPORT: DEEP TROUBLE!
22 PERSONNEL PROFILE: VIRGIL TRACY
24 VEHICLE DOSSIER: THUNDERBIRD 2
26 PUZZLES: BIG PROBLEMS!
27 PUZZLE: ALL ABOARD!
28 ACTIVITY: BUILD THUNDERBIRD 2
32 SECRET REPORT: NO WAY OUT?
34 PERSONNEL PROFILE: ALAN TRACY

36 VEHICLE DOSSIER: THUNDERBIRD 3
38 PUZZLES: SPACE PROBE!
39 PUZZLE: ROCK RECOVERY
40 SECRET REPORT: CABLE CLIMB
42 PERSONNEL PROFILE: GORDON TRACY
44 VEHICLE DOSSIER: THUNDERBIRD 4
46 PUZZLES: JOKER IN THE PACK!
47 PUZZLE: SEARCH AND RESCUE
48 GAME: SHORT CIRCUIT
50 PERSONNEL PROFILE: JOHN TRACY
52 VEHICLE DOSSIER: THUNDERBIRD 5
54 PUZZLE: WE HAVE A SITUATION!
55 MASTER OF DISGUISE: THE HOOD
56 PERSONNEL PROFILES: AWESOME ALLIES
58 QUIZ: WHICH TRACY BROTHER ARE YOU?
60 ACTIVITY: BADGE OF HONOUR
61 PUZZLE ANSWERS

INTERNAT

INTERNATIONAL RESCUE

When disaster strikes and people are in danger International Rescue is ready to help! From their secret island base and with their cutting-edge Thunderbird vehicles, the five fearless Tracy brothers, along with Kayo and Brains, pull off amazing feats of heroism. No rescue is too big and no journey too far to save a life.

TRACY ISLAND

International Rescue's secret base is on a remote island in the South Pacific Ocean. It may look like a luxury holiday home, but hidden underneath is a cave system formed by lava tubes. These caves house the Thunderbirds hangars and launch bays. Also underground is the lab used by Brains, the team's genius inventor.

SCOTT TRACY

Thunderbird 1

VIRGIL TRACY

Thunderbird 2

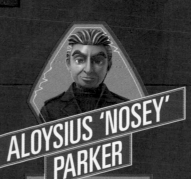

GORDON TRACY

Thunderbird 4

JOHN TRACY

Thunderbird 5

ALAN TRACY

Thunderbird 3

TANUSHA 'KAYO' KYRANO

Thunderbird S

BRAINS

Engineer

GRANDMA TRACY

Manager — Tracy Island

LADY PENELOPE CREIGHTON-WARD

International Rescue operative

ALOYSIUS 'NOSEY' PARKER

FAB 1 chauffeur

SCOTT TRACY

Scott is the oldest Tracy brother. Since his father went missing, he has been International Rescue's unofficial leader. Bold and fearless, he's ready for anything – whether it be jumping out of a plane backwards or diving into a lava-filled chasm!

DATA FILE

- Name .... Scott Tracy
- Craft .... Thunderbird 1
- Task .... First responder
- Special equipment ..... Jetpack and grapple launcher
- Key strengths .... Quick-thinking and great at making decisions
- Weakness .... Worries too much about past mistakes
- Most likely to say .... "We can handle it!"

1 SCOTT TRACY

F.A.B. FACT

Scott will stop at nothing for a mission, including sacrificing himself to save others. Thankfully, it hasn't come to that yet!

QUICK QUOTES

Here's what the team says about Scott

ALAN

"Scott's a great big brother. He'd do anything for us — and anything for a mission."

VIRGIL
"My advice to Scott? Take a few seconds to stop and think! Luckily for us, his instincts are usually right."

GORDON
"He sure is bossy, but I guess he always gets the job done! I just wish I could make him laugh..."

SCOTT IN ACTION!

The entire city of Taipei in Taiwan was in danger after earthquakes moved a solar-gathering satellite. Scott set off to adjust it, but he didn't bank on the rays frying his jetpack! When the satellite started breaking up, Scott used Thunderbird 1's remote control. He 'surfed' the falling debris off the edge of the satellite, landing safely on top of TB1.

F.A.B. FACT

As the first responder, Scott is usually the fastest to arrive in an emergency situation.

PENS TO THE RESCUE!

Be quick on the draw and give Scott some cool colours. Copy the main picture or give him a new look!

THUNDERBIRD 1

This super-fast craft can reach anywhere on the planet in 30 minutes or less – vital for a fast-response vehicle! This allows Thunderbird 1 pilot Scott Tracy to get to an emergency situation before anyone else and call for backup if necessary.

Cockpit

Avionics

Fold-back wings for vertical flight

Heat shielding

Variable flow intake and exhaust

VTOL hatch

ESSENTIAL INFO

SCOTT TRACY

- Craft .... Thunderbird 1
- Pilot .... Scott Tracy
- Function .... Fast-response vehicle
- Top speed .... 24,140 kph
- Maximum altitude .... 45.7 km
- Equipment .... Sonar, radar, radiation shielding and missile-defence alarm system

MISSION REPORT

Thanks to a rogue Artificial Intelligence, a runaway train was left hurtling straight for a major Japanese city. With no time to lose, Thunderbird 1 was the craft to call. Brains was the only person capable of fixing the train's complex power system, so Scott brought him along for the ride.

Scott flew alongside the speeding locomotive, releasing a grappling arm from a hatch in TB1's belly. Switching to autopilot, Scott secured Brains to the grappling arm and lowered him down to the train's hatch. After an alarming brush with a nearby mountain, Scott got the terrified Brains aboard the train to avert the disaster!

VEHICLE VITALS

Thunderbird 1 is stored in a specialized underground hangar on Tracy Island.

VEHICLE VITALS

Thunderbird 1 has a VTOL system — this stands for vertical take-off and landing.

5

4

3

2

1

11

MISSION LOG

Scott Tracy has completed a report on a recent mission. Well, he had until Gordon played a practical joke on him, deleting some of the words and replacing others with pictures! Can you help Scott fill in the blanks? Either say what you see in the picture or write down a word from the list – each word appears only once.

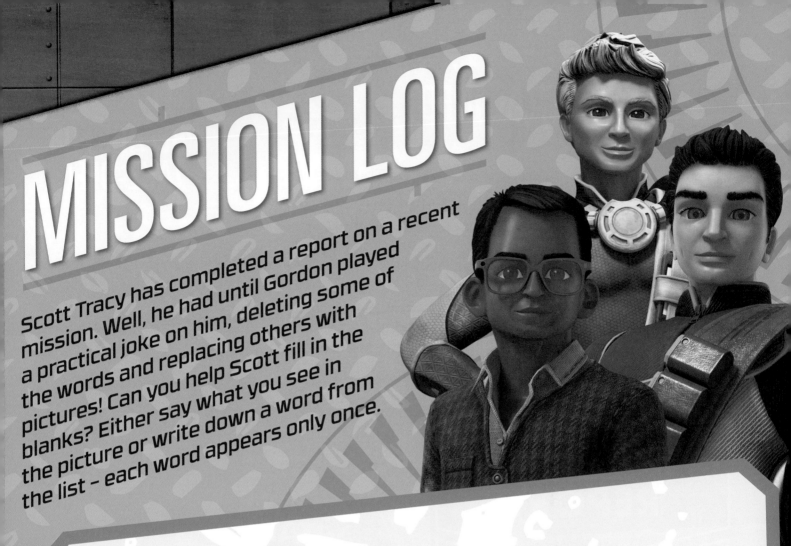

SCOTT TRACY REPORT

The mission began with a _ _ _ _ _ from . He alerted us to a runaway _ _ _ _ _ _ in Japan. told me to reset the power distribution. It was too big a task to take on _ _ _ _ _, so he came with me.

With on autopilot, I helped get down to the train. It turns out that he's not confident under _ _ _ _ _ _ _ _ _ _. Soon we were heading straight for a head-on collision with a huge _ _ _ _ _ _ _ _ _!

12

responded to my command immediately.

_____ averted! We still needed to _____ the train down, and fast! The trouble was the train computer had locked us out.

I tried to use [image] to slow the train. It worked, but my _____ went shooting off into the distance. [image] switched the train to a different track, but we had a new _____! We were heading straight for Unabara City's main terminal.

[image] realized that it wasn't a computer _____ that had locked us out. It was almost like the train was thinking for itself. [image] worked out that the computer wanted to play a _____! This helped [image] decide that he needed to distract the computer _____ enough for us to regain control of the train.

ANSWERS ON PAGE 61.

WORD LIST

CRISIS	GAME	VIRUS	LONG
CALL	MOUNTAIN	PRESSURE	SHIP
SOLO	TRAIN	SLOW	PROBLEM

BUILD THUNDERBIRD 1

Building a Thunderbird is an exciting challenge – just ask Brains! Based on the inventor's original blueprints, now you can construct your own magnificent model of Thunderbird 1. Can you handle it? Definitely!

YOU WILL NEED:
- Safety scissors
- Craft glue and stick
- Pencil

Always ask an adult for help when you use scissors.

INSTRUCTIONS

1. Carefully remove pages 15 and 16.

2. Cut out Part A and roll it into a cone. Glue down the tabs on the inside using the purple dots on both sides to show you where to place each tab.

3. Cut out Part B and roll it into a tube. Glue down the tabs on the inside using the green dots to help you.

4. Glue Part A to Part B using the tabs. Use the coloured dots to help you.

5. Cut out Part C and roll it into a tube. Glue down the tabs on the inside using the pink dots to help you. Glue Part C to Part B.

6. Cut out Parts D and E and roll each part back on itself. Glue down the tabs on the inside using the coloured dots to help you.

7. Glue Parts D and E to the side of Part C using the tabs.

TURN TO PAGE 17

J

C

B

F

A

G

D

E

I

H

K

16

INSTRUCTIONS (CONTINUED)

8. Cut out Part F. Roll it into a cone and glue down the tab.

9. Cut out Part G and roll it into a tube and glue down the tabs. Then glue the tabs at the top to the inside of Part F.

10. Cut out Part H and glue together using green dots to help you. Glue the bottom tabs of Part G to the inside of Part H. This completes the middle section.

11. Cut out Part I. Fold each of the four rear engines into box shapes using the picture as a guide. Glue the tabs in place using the coloured dots to help you.

12. Cut out Part J, roll it into a tube and glue together. Glue the bottom tabs to the base of Part I. When dry, glue the engine boxes to the side of Part J. This completes the bottom section.

13. Glue the bottom section to the middle section and then the middle section to the top section, using the tabs.

14. Finally, cut out Parts K and glue them to the engines.

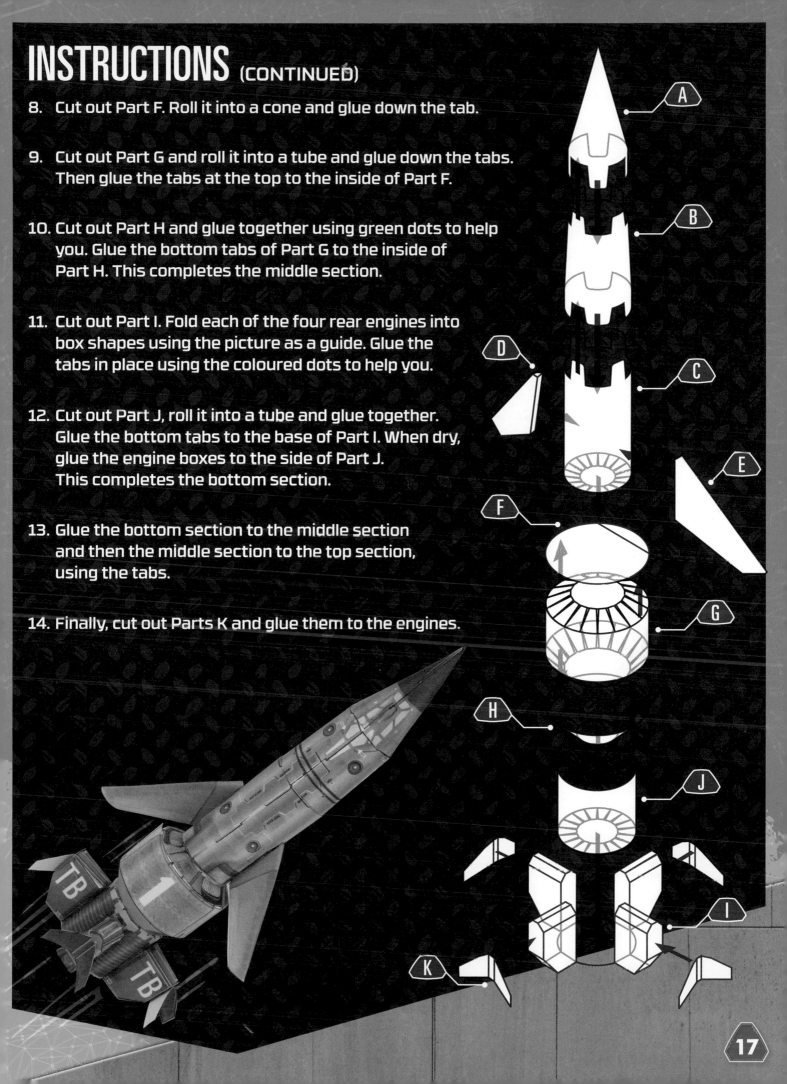

CODE CONFUSION

The Tracy brothers sometimes use code on secret missions. Unfortunately, the decoding device on board Thunderbird 1 is broken and Scott must work out the message below himself. Using the key, can you work out who needs his help and where they are?

KEY

A	B	C
D	E	F
G	H	I
J	K	L
M	N	O
P	Q	R
S	T	U
V	W	X
Y	Z	.

18

FAST RESPONSE

A group of explorers is missing in the Sahara Desert – without any food or water. How quickly can you guide Thunderbird 1 through the sandstorm to their camp?

START

ANSWER ON PAGE 61.

FINISH

DEEP TROUBLE!

International Rescue faces a race against time to save millions of lives.

It was another normal day in zero gravity for John Tracy! That's until he spotted a dangerous increase in the radiation readings over South Africa. It looked like a mission for International Rescue!

John continued to monitor the situation from Thunderbird 5, while his brothers Scott and Virgil suited up on Tracy Island.

It was unclear what was causing the radiation. After all, nuclear power hadn't been used in decades and there was no sign of an explosion.

RADIATION RIDDLE

The two pilots took to the skies. Virgil reckoned he was carrying everything they would ever need in Thunderbird 2, including the kitchen sink! Scott took advantage of Thunderbird 1's speed and went ahead to check out the situation.

There was no sign of an explosion.

"You're right on top of it, Thunderbird 1," warned John on a comms link. As Scott pulled Thunderbird 1 round for another pass, he spotted an old uranium mine. John reckoned that it must have been reopened – and needed sealing fast!

Brains called Scott with a timely warning about radiation. "Where you are right now there's approximately 4,953 times the safe amount in the air... give or take," the inventor said.

60

Brains reassured him that the radiation shielding on his suit would protect him for a while. He just shouldn't hang around for too long! "Keep an eye on your Geiger counter," Brains said. "If it strays into the red, get out fast – or you'll end up crispier than Grandma's meat loaf!"

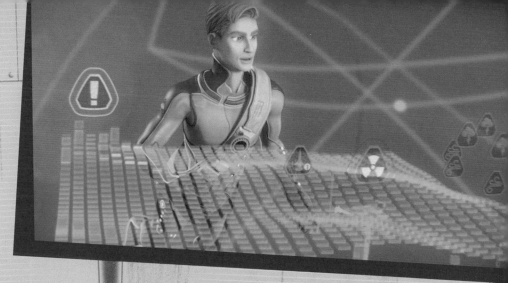

MINE OF INFORMATION

Scott found that the computer system had come back online and the main hatch to the mine was open. He incorrectly guessed it was a short circuit. Meanwhile, John had found some background details. The mine was part of a huge uranium extraction operation, but it had closed down 20 years ago in 2040.

Scott was about to seal the main hatch. Then he noticed one of the radiation suits was missing – and there were fresh footsteps in the dust. "Someone's down there!" he cried. There was only one thing for it – he was going in! There was no time to wait for Virgil. The intruder might not know how much danger they were facing.

"Someone's down there!" Scott cried.

DESCENT INTO DANGER

John warned that there were only 15 minutes to get in and out before the radiation would cause an ecological disaster. There might be even less time, as a huge storm was getting near. International Rescue couldn't risk fallout over downtown Pretoria – more than 12 million people would be in danger!

More than 12 million people would be in danger!

The elevator to the mine wasn't responding and the depth of the shaft was hard to guess. Using his handy grappling launcher, Scott quickly descended hundreds of metres. Unfortunately, he was fast running out of grapple packs. He spotted a ledge with a tunnel entrance and swung towards it – when someone in a metal mech suit suddenly cut his line!

He desperately flung his arms out to grab the ledge, but fell into the darkness below...

TURN TO PAGE **32**

VIRGIL TRACY

He looks like an all-action tough guy, although Virgil also has a softer side! He's the biggest and strongest of the Tracy brothers. Careful and level-headed, Virgil is a useful guy to have in any emergency.

DATA FILE

● Name	Virgil Tracy
● Craft	Thunderbird 2
● Duties	Demolition, heavy lifting and transport
● Special equipment	Mechanical grasping arms called the Jaws of Life, used for cutting and clearing work
● Key strength	Calm in a crisis
● Weakness	Sometimes forgets his own strength
● Most likely to say	"Time for some heavy lifting!"

F.A.B. FACT

Virgil doesn't like waiting for orders. But his impatience usually pays off, as it means he's close at hand when needed most!

QUICK QUOTES

Here's what the team says about Virgil

GORDON

"He keeps us all in check. Best keep him away from mountain missions, though — that voice could start an avalanche!"

SCOTT

"When I needed help escaping from a crumbling uranium mine, Virgil was there. He delivers — every time."

LADY PENELOPE

"Although I'm quite capable of looking after myself, Virgil did help me escape a collapsing temple!"

BOX CLEVER

Virgil is a talented artist – and you can be, too! Copy each box into the grid to draw a picture of the Thunderbird 2 pilot.

VIRGIL IN ACTION!

A dangerous anti-tech group called the Luddites tried to disable all electrical devices. An unlikely partnership went to stop them – Virgil and Grandma Tracy! Grandma proved to be an ideal decoy, allowing Virgil to bring the roof crashing down on the villains' deadly device!

THUNDERBIRD 2

The massive Thunderbird 2 is like a factory with wings! The centre section can separate from the rest of the vehicle. Inside are custom-built P.O.D.s, which are put together in minutes. P.O.D.s can be fitted with various devices, from jet engines and laser cutters to skis and grappling arms!

In-flight refuelling nozzle

Communications and sensors

Super-charged intake system

High-speed manoeuvre flaps

Cargo bay P.O.D.-assembly factory

Vertical take-off and landing (VTOL) thrusters

Primary-thrust nozzles

ESSENTIAL INFO

- Craft .... Thunderbird 2
- Pilot .... Virgil Tracy
- Function .... Backup equipment transport
- Top speed .... 8,050 kph
- Maximum altitude .... 30.5 km
- Equipment .... On-board P.O.D. assembly factory and instant fabrication machines, which can build almost any tool imaginable!

MISSION REPORT

Thunderbird 2 came in very useful rescuing Kayo from a supersonic airliner with sabotaged landing gear! The P.O.D. assembly factory on board TB2 built two vehicles to act as wheels for the plane. Gordon and Alan were inside the P.O.D.s, but had to abort when the weight of the mammoth airliner almost crushed them.

Virgil quickly came up with another plan. Expertly flying TB2 underneath and activating the VTOL engines, he gave the plane a piggyback ride to safety. Neat!

VEHICLE VITALS

Thunderbird 2 has a vertical take-off and landing (VTOL) system, like TB1. As long as the area is large enough, TB2 is able to hover over water and land anywhere!

VEHICLE VITALS

Thunderbird 2 is the perfect craft for heavy lifting. It can carry just over 100 tonnes!

BIG PROBLEMS!

Virgil Tracy transports equipment far and wide in Thunderbird 2. See how far your brainpower gets you solving these two missions!

PIECE OF THE ACTION!

Which three puzzle pieces complete this picture of Virgil?

A

B

C

D

E

F

1

2

3

DELIVERY DILEMMA

Virgil has three pieces of kit to deliver. Can you work out who needs each item and at what time Virgil will deliver it?

🔻 Virgil must visit Brains first. He's delivering something for repair, but collecting a jetpack to deliver later today.

🔻 Alan is not expecting a torpedo.

🔻 The gyroscope will be dropped off exactly three hours before the jetpack.

🔻 The torpedo will be delivered last.

Gyroscope	Alan
Jetpack	Brains
Torpedo	Gordon

TIME	ITEM	PERSON
09:00		
12:00		
15:00		

ANSWERS ON PAGE 61.

ALL ABOARD!

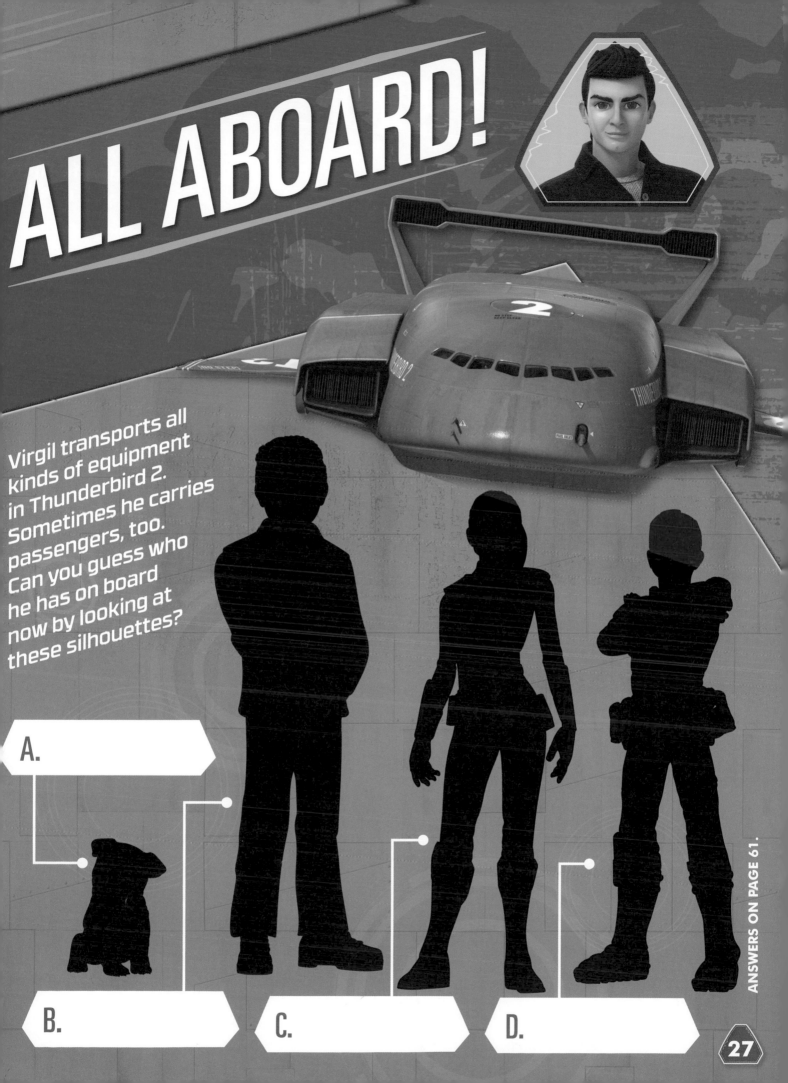

Virgil transports all kinds of equipment in Thunderbird 2. Sometimes he carries passengers, too. Can you guess who he has on board now by looking at these silhouettes?

A.

B.

C.

D.

ANSWERS ON PAGE 61.

BUILD THUNDERBIRD 2

Thunderbird 2 can land almost anywhere. Now it's coming to your home! Cut out and construct this model to have your own mini version of Virgil's cool craft.

YOU WILL NEED:
- Safety scissors
- Glue

Always ask an adult for help if you need it.

INSTRUCTIONS

1. Carefully cut out all the parts.

2. Take Part A and start assembling the front. Fold down the front piece, glue the tab and stick it to the next piece as shown on the diagram. This is the underside of the nose.

3. Take the other nose pieces, curl them under, glue their tabs and stick them to the nose base.

4. Work your way along the sides by rolling the side edge tabs underneath and sticking them in place.

5. Stop when you get to the last 3 pieces of the module. You will glue these together later.

6. Take Part B. Fold along the grey lines. Glue the tabs and attach them to their correct places by matching up the colours.

TURN TO PAGE 31

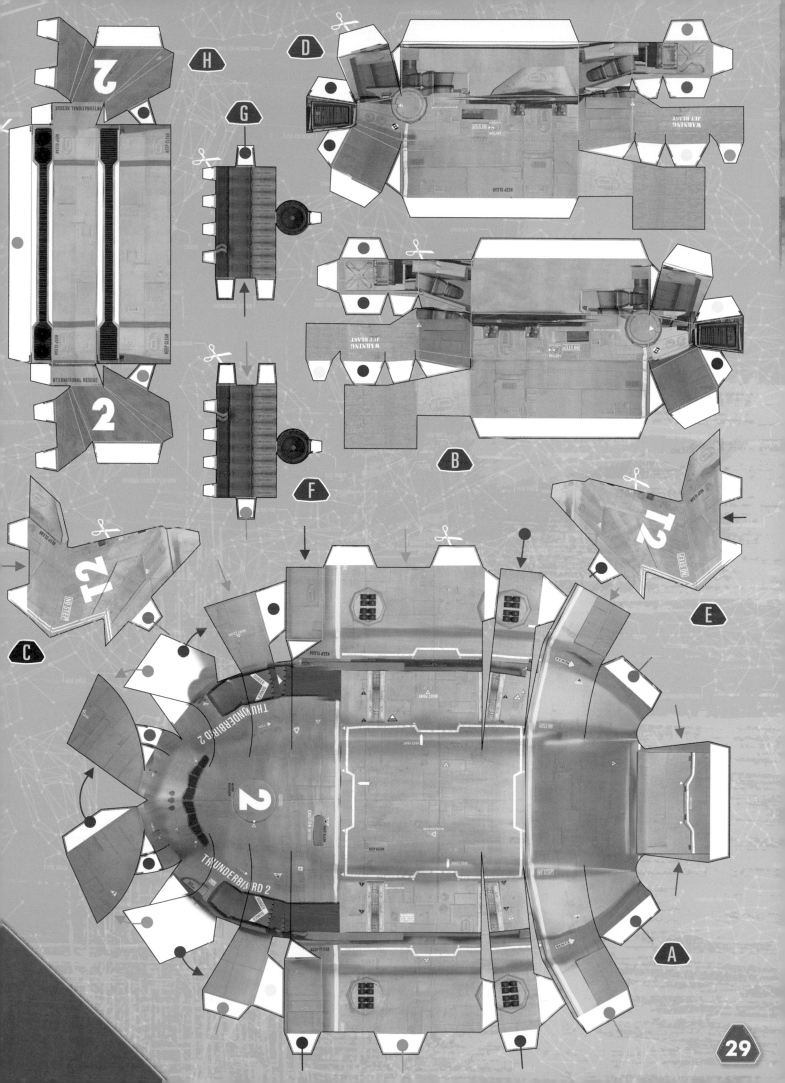

29

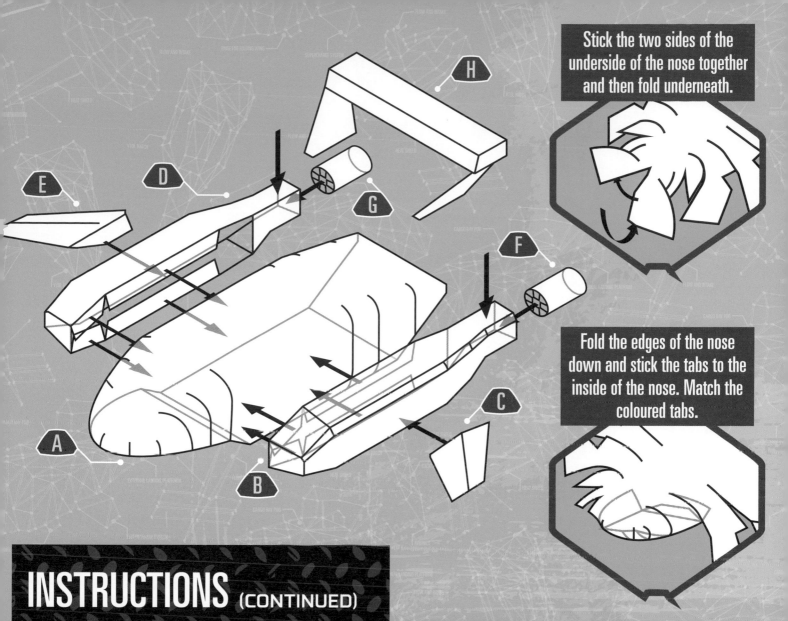

Stick the two sides of the underside of the nose together and then fold underneath.

Fold the edges of the nose down and stick the tabs to the inside of the nose. Match the coloured tabs.

INSTRUCTIONS (CONTINUED)

7. Take Part C. Fold along the grey lines. Glue the tabs and stick this piece together so that it lies flat. This is the wing. Attach it to the bottom of Part B as shown in the diagram.

8. Repeat steps 6 and 7 for Parts D and E.

9. Take Parts B and D and glue them to Part A where shown in the diagram. You can put your fingers inside the P.O.D. to help with the sticking.

10. Finish assembling Part A by folding the back end down and gluing it to the edge tabs. Glue the tab of the back end to the P.O.D.

11. Roll Part F into a tube and stick the edges together using the tabs. Fold the cap down and stick its tab inside the end. Fold down the four tabs on the other end and attach them to the end of Part B as shown in the diagram. Repeat with Part G and attach it to Part D.

12. Make the tail by taking Part H and folding and gluing the two side struts like you did with the wings. Fold the engine into a long box by sticking the tabs. Fold down the two ends and attach the struts to the end of Parts B and D as indicated by the arrows.

NO WAY OUT?

Trapped in a uranium mine, Scott's luck is at rock bottom...

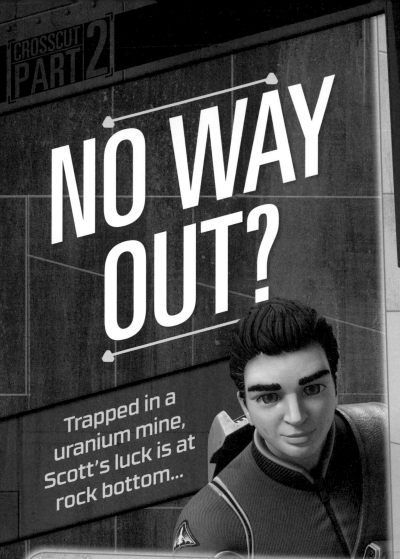

Thunderbird 2 landed close to the mine entrance. "Everything alright down there?" said Virgil into his radio. But Scott was slowly waking up after his fall. He suddenly realized that someone in a huge mech suit was carrying him – and he was about to be locked in a cage!

His survival instinct took over just in time, and Scott escaped from his captor's grip. He tried to reason with whoever was inside the suit... whilst dodging metal claws! John was worried. "Thunderbird 1, what's happening?" he asked. "Apparently, our intruder doesn't play well with others!" retorted Scott, dodging another blow.

INTRUDER ALERT!

Realizing action was better than talking, Scott jumped onto his attacker. He spun his opponent around, but the mech suit fell on top of Scott, pinning him to the floor. As the suit opened, a woman stepped out. She wasn't happy, especially when Scott accused her of stealing. She claimed to be taking back what belonged to her. Leaving the eldest Tracy brother trapped, she made for the mine entrance with her huge haul of refined uranium.

Scott warned her that she had overloaded the elevator. He was proved right when the gears made a terrible noise and the platform plunged down. Scott used his last remaining grapple rope to catch the mysterious woman before she crashed to the ground.

John was alarmed to see the radiation levels were increasing even faster. It was no wonder with the state of the broken uranium storage capsules!

Radiation levels were dangerously high.

Back underground, the mystery woman revealed she was Marion Von Arkel, whose family once owned the mine. She wasn't grateful for being saved, blaming Scott for the elevator malfunction. The pair were busy rowing when Virgil interrupted. "Right now we have to figure a way to get you out of there before your organs get microwaved!" he said.

SECRET BUYER

Scott was concerned that Marion was like the uranium – unstable. He was right not to trust her. Marion had secretly stashed a couple of uranium canisters in her backpack and was disappearing into a tunnel. Having grown up at the mine, she knew another way out!

Marion wasn't happy that the world was no longer reliant on nuclear power. She was planning to sell the remaining uranium to restore her family's fortunes. She had received an offer she couldn't refuse – Scott knew it must be from The Hood!

As they ran up an old metal staircase, arguing as they went, Marion didn't notice the steps had rusted away... Scott grabbed her, saving her from a fatal fall. There was no way up, no time to go down and radiation levels were getting dangerously high. It was time to call for help. Scott opened his comms link. "Thunderbird 2? We have a problem!"

TURN TO PAGE 40

ALAN TRACY

The youngest Tracy brother certainly can fly a rocket! Teenager Alan operates the complex Thunderbird 3. He manages to pull off incredible feats of aerial acrobatics without breaking a sweat.

DATA FILE

Name	Alan Tracy
Craft	Thunderbird 3
Duty	Astronaut
Special equipment	Gravity rockets and portable life-support system
Key strength	Brilliant pilot with amazing reflexes
Weaknesses	Sometimes makes mistakes – and likes to sleep in!
Most likely to say	"Piece of cake!"

3 ALAN TRACY

F.A.B. FACT

When he's off duty, Alan relaxes by playing video games and watching old kung fu movies.

ACCESS

QUICK QUOTES

Here's what the team says about Alan

KAYO

"Alan had trouble deactivating The Hood's satellite — until I told him it was just like fixing a TV."

GRANDMA TRACY

"I think Alan might be an even better pilot than his dad. He doesn't score highly for housekeeping, though!"

JOHN

"If it's a morning mission, wake him early. The last time he got up in a hurry, he ended up in the closet!"

ALAN IN ACTION!

Rescuing a miner from an asteroid seemed routine for Alan and Kayo in Thunderbird 3. But when they crash-landed, they had to use explosives to stop the asteroid heading straight for the Sun. Alan then had the bright idea of using more explosives to relaunch TB3 into space!

ALL ALANS

How many times does the name ALAN appear in a straight line in the grid below? It can be horizontal or vertical and run forwards or backwards.

A	L	A	N
L	N	L	A
A	L	A	L
N	A	L	A

ANSWER ON PAGE 61.

F.A.B. FACT

Alan doesn't always stay in TB3 — he uses a jet-propelled board to travel around in space.

THUNDERBIRD 3

If help is needed in Earth's orbit or beyond, IR calls in Thunderbird 3, flown by daredevil pilot Alan Tracy. TB3 has three support struts that convert into stabilizing arms. These are ideal for grabbing onto passing asteroids and off-course satellites!

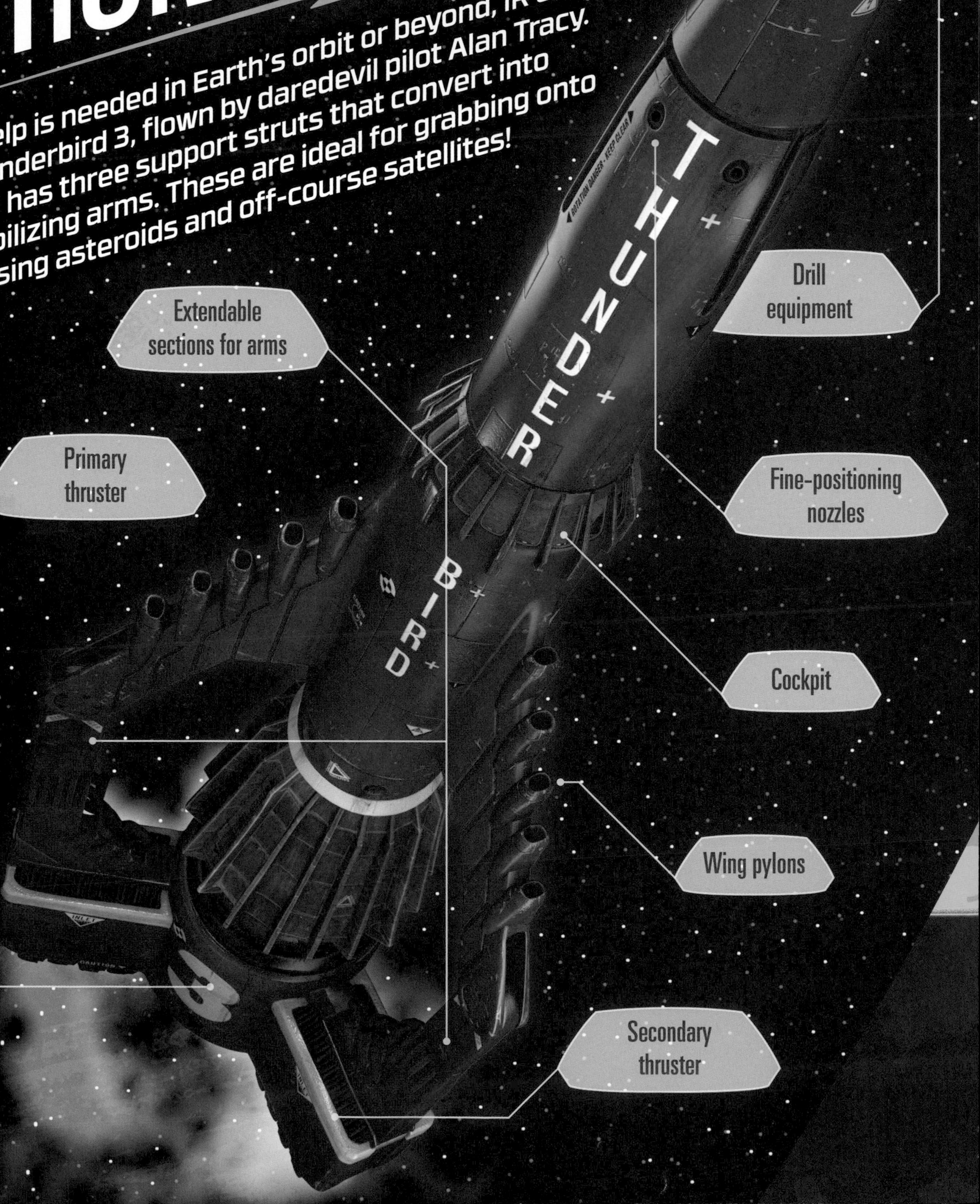

Extendable sections for arms

Drill equipment

Primary thruster

Fine-positioning nozzles

Cockpit

Wing pylons

Secondary thruster

ESSENTIAL INFO

Craft	Thunderbird 3
Pilot	Alan Tracy
Function	Space rescue and carrying equipment
Top acceleration	10 g
Maximum altitude	The Universe is the limit!
Equipment	Tri-grasping arms, interchangeable cargo section and highly advanced radiation shielding

MISSION REPORT

Thunderbird 3 once had a terrifying encounter with an explosive orbital mine! A relic of the Global Conflict of 2020, the nuclear-powered device was programmed to explode if it left Earth's orbit. So pilot Alan Tracy got the mine to lock in with his craft's movements by activating TB3's ion-fusion engines.

Playing a deadly game of cat and mouse, Alan completed a series of awesome manoeuvres. Finally, the kill code was found and the mine shut down – close call!

VEHICLE VITALS

The grappling arms on TB3 are great at grabbing garbage when Alan is on 'space junk' duty!

VEHICLE VITALS

The centre capsule can be changed to give Thunderbird 3 extra payload capacity. The central section holds P.O.D.s for space rescue.

37

SPACE PROBE!

Alan Tracy often reckons he has all the answers. Prove that you do, too, by solving these tricky teasers!

ALAN ALERT

An imposter is pretending to be Alan, but Brains has spotted the fake. Can you find five differences between the two images?

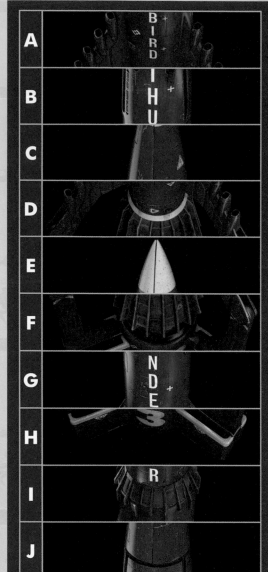

WRONG ROCKET

This Thunderbird 3 picture has been scrambled. Can you put the pieces in the correct order?

FACT OR FIB?

ARE YOU AN EXPERT ON THE THUNDERBIRD 3 PILOT? JUST SAY WHETHER THE FOLLOWING STATEMENTS ARE TRUE OR FALSE...

1 Alan Tracy is a talented astronaut.

2 He hates watching kung fu movies.

3 Alan enjoys spending time with Yako.

4 He is the youngest Tracy brother.

5 Alan loves to sleep!

Answers on page 61.

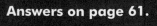

ROCK RECOVERY

Thunderbird 3 is on its way to dock with Thunderbird 5. Can you help Alan guide his rocket safely through the asteroid field?

START

FINISH

ANSWER ON PAGE 61.

CABLE CLIMB

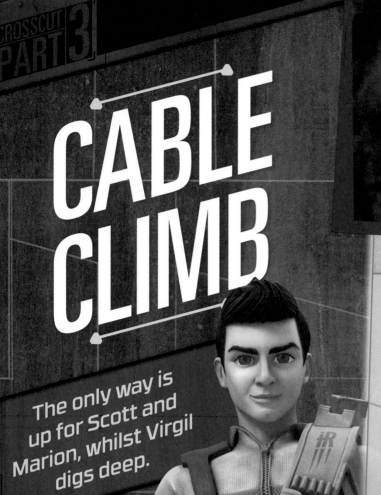

The only way is up for Scott and Marion, whilst Virgil digs deep.

Virgil wanted to rescue them from the mine. Scott told him it was too dangerous – he didn't want anyone else exposed to the radiation. And besides, he'd come up with a plan of his own. The first step was to remote pilot Thunderbird 1 just above the mine.

Virgil decided to start his own backup plan. In Thunderbird 2's factory module, he fitted the components for a Mole P.O.D. Then he drilled into the ground with the P.O.D., disappearing in a shower of earth.

STAIRCASE TO SAFETY?

Meanwhile, Thunderbird 1 lifted the outside hatch clean off before dropping a magnet on a cable into the shaft. Scott finally managed to grab it and attach it to the staircase. As the cable started to wind up, Scott and Marion kicked at a weak point and clung onto the loose set of stairs.

John radioed in to say the storm wasn't on its way any more – it had already arrived! Thunderbird 1 shook in the strong winds, which meant Scott and Marion were bashed against the sides of the mine shaft! When the cable got wedged between some rocks, Scott realized they would have to start climbing.

John had sealed off the main entrance, but the broken storage capsules meant radiation was still leaking from the other hatch. Scott knew this meant Pretoria still wasn't safe. He told Virgil to bury them in the mine if they weren't out in five minutes!

SECONDS FROM DISASTER

The trapped pair continued to climb, but Marion was struggling with her backpack. Scott knew exactly what she had in it. "You'd find it easier if you dumped the uranium…" he advised. "You don't want it in the wrong hands any more than I do!"

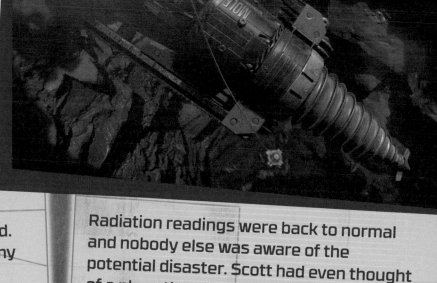

Marion tried to climb, but lost her grip!

Marion tried to climb, but lost her grip. Dangling with one hand, she clutched the backpack with the other. Its weight pulled her from the cable. The uranium disappeared down the shaft, but Scott grabbed Marion just in time!

But their troubles weren't over yet. Thunderbird 1 was hit by the storm-force winds. It caused the cable to jerk and fling the unlucky pair back down into the abyss! Luckily, their landing was far softer than expected – Virgil's Mole P.O.D. was in the perfect position to catch them!

Back on the surface, International Rescue sealed up the mine forever.

Radiation readings were back to normal and nobody else was aware of the potential disaster. Scott had even thought of a place that needed Marion's expertise – the Global Defence Force could always use a nuclear-materials expert.

Now the only problem was what to do about Marion's buyer. He was expecting a delivery of refined uranium. Scott decided to send something picked up from the control-room floor. It was just a shame he wouldn't get to see The Hood's face when he took delivery of an old hamburger box!

END

GORDON TRACY

Wisecracking Gordon is the joker of the Tracy brothers. He lives life to the full and loves to have fun. Gordon is responsible for patrolling the ocean depths in Thunderbird 4. At least that's one thing he takes seriously!

DATA FILE

- Name .... Gordon Tracy
- Craft .... Thunderbird 4
- Duty .... Underwater search and rescue
- Special equipment .... Aqua scooter and heavy-duty breathing apparatus
- Key strength .... Stays focused on a mission
- Weakness .... Some of his jokes are awful!
- Most likely to say .... "My squid-sense is tingling!"

4 GORDON TRACY

F.A.B. FACT

Gordon is always giving Lady Penelope a hard time, but he likes her more than he would admit!

QUICK QUOTES

Here's what the team says about Gordon

ALAN

"Gordon's jokes belong in his natural habitat — at the bottom of the ocean!"

VIRGIL

"I sometimes travel with Gordon when TB4 is docked inside Thunderbird 2. My brother makes a great co-pilot."

PARKER

"I think Lady Penelope gets annoyed with his jokes. If you ask me, I reckon she quite likes the young chap!"

POOCH PRANK

Gordon is playing a joke on Lady Penelope. He's hidden Sherbert and has left clues and a map to his location. Help her find her missing dog.

	A	B	C	D	E
1	START				
2					
3					
4					
5					

GORDON IN ACTION!

Gordon once got trapped inside an ancient pyramid with Lady Penelope and Parker. The hazards they faced included flooded tunnels and deadly toxic gas. Using their wits and Gordon's mini spear gun, they survived until Thunderbird 2 rescued them.

1 Go *EAST* three spaces

2 Go *SOUTH* one space

3 Move *WEST* one space

4 Go *SOUTH* two spaces

5 Move *EAST* one space

LOCATION

ANSWER ON PAGE 61.

THUNDERBIRD 4

The smallest of the Tracys' vehicles, Thunderbird 4 is mainly used for deep-sea missions. But this speedy submersible is not only great underwater – it can also travel over land on hoverjets. TB4's mechanical arms make light work of clearing shipwrecks and toxic waste.

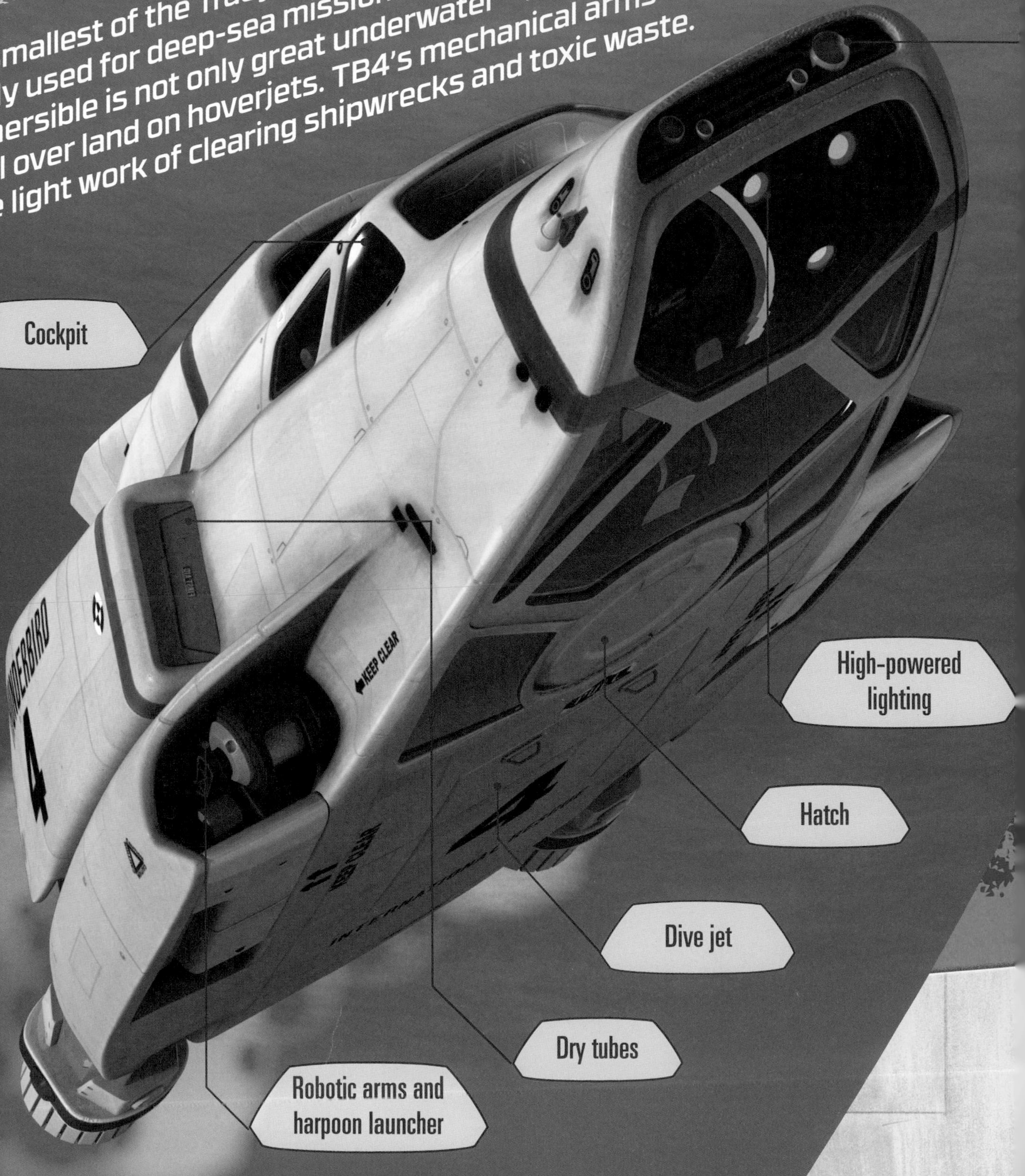

Scanning array

Cockpit

High-powered lighting

Hatch

Dive jet

Dry tubes

Robotic arms and harpoon launcher

KEEP CLEAR

THUNDERBIRD 4

ESSENTIAL INFO

GORDON TRACY
THUNDERBIRDS 4

- Craft .... Thunderbird 4
- Pilot .... Gordon Tracy
- Function .... Underwater search and rescue
- Underwater speed .... 295 kph
- Maximum operating depth .... 9.1 km
- Equipment .... Active 4D sonar array, adaptive utility arms, demolition torpedoes and quick-launch escape tubes

5

4

MISSION REPORT

A crisis began when a defective Hadron Collider created a gravity well. Soon planes were being sucked out of the sky! Thunderbird 4 was the only craft that could stand up to its intense forces and was lowered into the well via a cable attached to TB2.

After a hair-raising ride, Gordon landed Thunderbird 4, pushed a button on his gauntlet and blasted the generator with torpedoes. Gravity was restored to normal, a space station was spared from burn-up and all lives were saved!

VEHICLE VITALS

The lightning-quick Thunderbird 4 can reach the deepest depths in a few minutes, thanks to its reinforced hull and pressurized cabin.

3

2

VEHICLE VITALS

Thunderbird 4's robotic arms proved 'handy' when it rescued the team of an underwater research station.

1

JOKER IN THE PACK!

Gordon Tracy has a wicked sense of humour. Will you be smiling after tackling these missions?

NAME GAME

Gordon has been having fun with anagrams. Can you unscramble the letters and find four of these five members of IR? Whose name does not appear?

1. LEAN EYED PLOP
2. CATS CRY TOT
3. MANGY RAT CARD
4. CART GIRL IVY

Something fishy is going on! Gordon has made six changes to the second picture of Thunderbird 4 – how quickly can you spot them?

SEARCH AND RESCUE

Gordon Tracy spends a lot of time underwater. Today he's on a personal mission – two relatives are lost at sea!

First, search out the watery words listed below and locate them in this grid. Words can read vertically, horizontally or diagonally in any direction.

The unused letters read from left to right, top to bottom will spell out the names of the duo in danger!

E	S	R	O	H	A	E	S	W	V
D	I	U	R	L	L	E	H	S	G
O	R	I	B	L	A	A	A	N	A
L	E	O	D	M	L	G	R	M	N
P	V	C	R	E	A	A	K	A	E
H	I	T	B	C	O	R	A	L	M
I	D	O	E	D	I	T	I	C	O
N	A	P	N	W	A	V	E	N	N
T	D	U	E	L	T	R	U	T	E
M	A	S	T	A	R	F	I	S	H

ANSWERS ON PAGE 61.

- ANEMONE
- BOAT
- CLAM
- CORAL
- DIVER
- DOLPHIN
- OCTOPUS
- SEAHORSE
- SHARK
- SHELL
- STARFISH
- SUBMARINE
- TIDE
- TURTLE
- WAVE
- WHALE

GORDON IS RESCUING _____ _____

47

SHORT CIRCUIT

Work together to help the Tracy brothers race home before it's too late!

Brains has sent out a distress signal. His robot helper, M.A.X., has gone haywire! The Tracy brothers all need to return home before M.A.X. breaks six important circuits that control the island's comms network. You're in this together — you will either all win or all lose!

YOU WILL NEED:

- 2-5 players
- 1 dice
- 5 character counters
- 6 circuit tokens

Use the tokens on the right or make your own.

INSTRUCTIONS

- Each player picks a character counter and places it on START. Any unused character counters and all six circuit tokens are placed on Tracy Island.

- Roll a dice to decide who goes first.

- Take it in turns to roll the dice and move your character up the board, following any instructions that you land on.

- Once during each game, each player can force another to move the number he or she has just rolled. Remember – each player can do this once only!

- If all the brothers make it to Tracy Island before the last circuit is removed and broken by M.A.X., you win!

If all the circuits are taken off the board first, everyone loses!

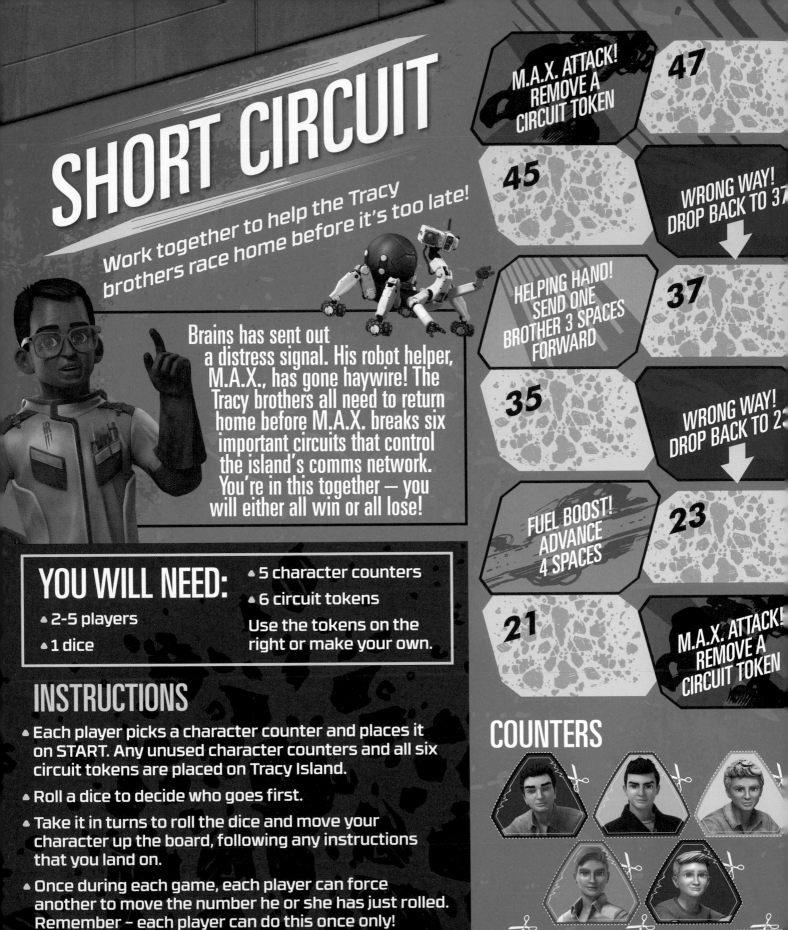

M.A.X. ATTACK! REMOVE A CIRCUIT TOKEN

47

45

WRONG WAY! DROP BACK TO 37

HELPING HAND! SEND ONE BROTHER 3 SPACES FORWARD

37

35

WRONG WAY! DROP BACK TO 23

FUEL BOOST! ADVANCE 4 SPACES

23

21

M.A.X. ATTACK! REMOVE A CIRCUIT TOKEN

COUNTERS

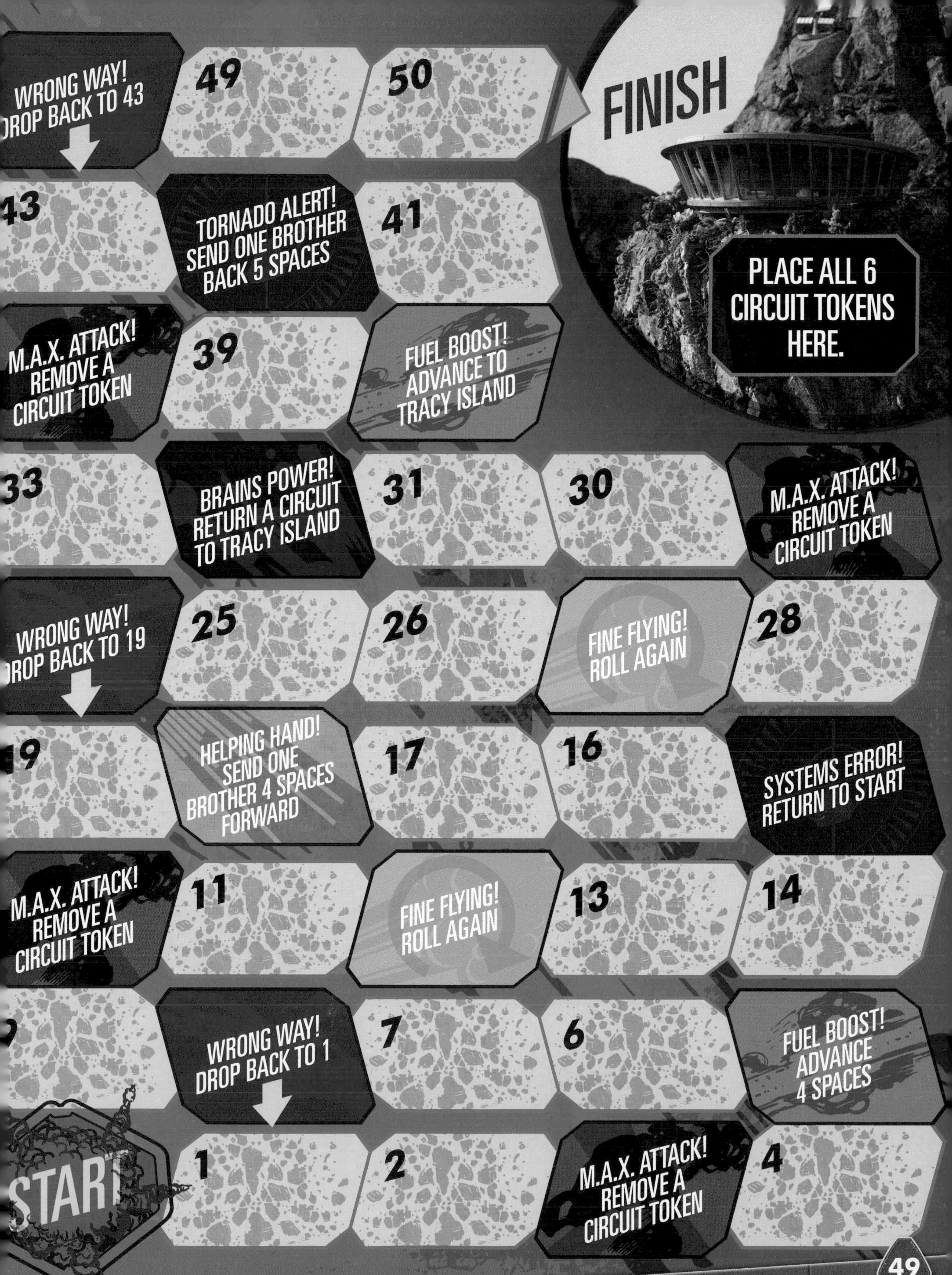

WRONG WAY! DROP BACK TO 43

49

50

FINISH

43

TORNADO ALERT! SEND ONE BROTHER BACK 5 SPACES

41

PLACE ALL 6 CIRCUIT TOKENS HERE.

M.A.X. ATTACK! REMOVE A CIRCUIT TOKEN

39

FUEL BOOST! ADVANCE TO TRACY ISLAND

33

BRAINS POWER! RETURN A CIRCUIT TO TRACY ISLAND

31

30

M.A.X. ATTACK! REMOVE A CIRCUIT TOKEN

WRONG WAY! DROP BACK TO 19

25

26

FINE FLYING! ROLL AGAIN

28

19

HELPING HAND! SEND ONE BROTHER 4 SPACES FORWARD

17

16

SYSTEMS ERROR! RETURN TO START

M.A.X. ATTACK! REMOVE A CIRCUIT TOKEN

11

FINE FLYING! ROLL AGAIN

13

14

WRONG WAY! DROP BACK TO 1

7

6

FUEL BOOST! ADVANCE 4 SPACES

START

1

2

M.A.X. ATTACK! REMOVE A CIRCUIT TOKEN

4

JOHN TRACY

John runs the International Rescue space station. He scans all frequencies on Earth, looking for problems that require IR's help. John is happiest in space and doesn't like being stuck on Tracy Island for too long.

DATA FILE

- **Name** .... John Tracy
- **Craft** .... Thunderbird 5
- **Duties** .... Space command, communications and dispatch
- **Special equipment** .... Rocket boots
- **Key strengths** .... Master of multi-tasking and easily copes with pressure
- **Weakness** .... Can become obsessed by one task
- **Most likely to say** .... "International Rescue, we have a situation!"

F.A.B. FACT

A fake "John" once fooled the Tracy brothers. However, they realized it was an imposter when "John" said he liked Grandma Tracy's cookies. The real John would never say that!

50

QUICK QUOTES

Here's what the team says about John

SCOTT
"John does a great job up there. He's usually the first to spot trouble on Earth — and then sends me there!"

LADY PENELOPE
"John's not very good at charades. He tried to mime he was in trouble, but I thought he was doing a dance!"

ALAN
"John's usually calm, but if you bug him on TB5, he may threaten you with 'sudden unexplained airlock failure'!"

COMMS CONUNDRUM

John's communications feeds have been sabotaged. Which line leads to the base on Tracy Island?

A   B   C   D   E

JOHN IN ACTION!

A rogue AI called Eos once took control of Thunderbird 5. With false messages being fed back to his brothers, John had to use his wits to stay alive as his air supply ran out. Rescued by Alan, John then reasoned with Eos and persuaded the advanced tech they could work together.

ANSWERS ON PAGE 61.

THUNDERBIRD 5

Space station Thunderbird 5 is International Rescue's all-seeing eye in the sky. Manned by John Tracy, its advanced systems listen in to communications and scan the globe for dangerous situations.

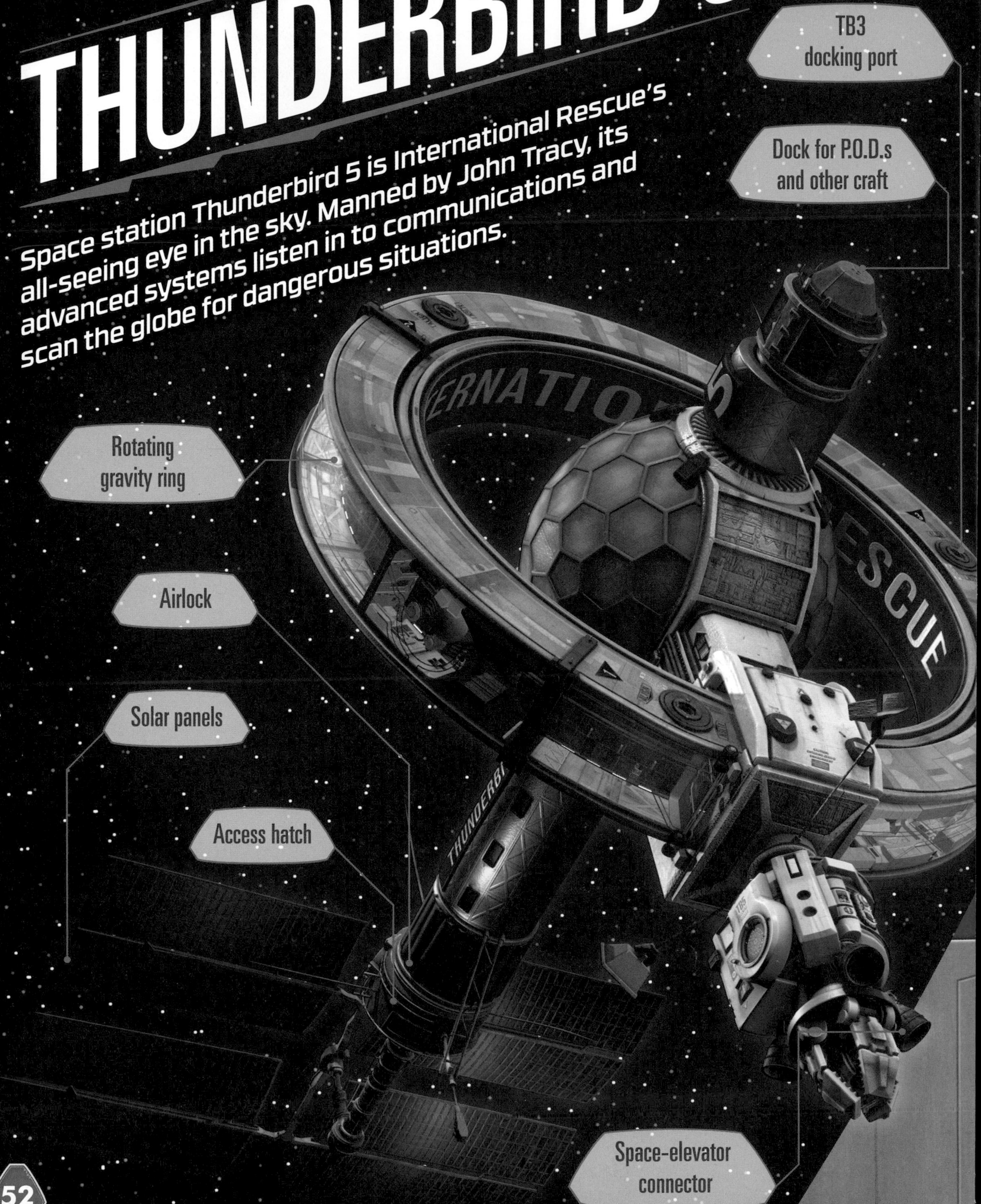

TB3 docking port

Dock for P.O.D.s and other craft

Rotating gravity ring

Airlock

Solar panels

Access hatch

Space-elevator connector

ESSENTIAL INFO

- Craft .... Thunderbird 5
- Pilot .... John Tracy
- Function .... Communications and logistics centre
- Reception range .... 161 million km
- Standard orbital altitude .... 54,000 km
- Equipment .... Audio and visual communications array, 365° holo-screens, space elevator to Tracy Island and adaptable P.O.D. vehicle

MISSION REPORT

Thunderbird 5 was needed to rescue the crew of the damaged CIRRUS weather station. Using its powerful thrusters, John positioned TB5 directly above CIRRUS. With split-second timing, he latched onto CIRRUS using the space elevator's cable and mooring claw.

John managed to wrap the nano-cable around TB5's enormous gravity ring. He then spun the gravity ring round and round, reeling in the nano-cable with CIRRUS on the end!

VEHICLE VITALS

The huge structure of Thunderbird 5 is linked to Tracy Island via a carbon nano-cable space elevator. It takes John just eight minutes to travel from Earth to TB5!

VEHICLE VITALS

Thunderbird 5 can change orbit and go on rescue missions itself — should the need arise.

WE HAVE A SITUATION!

Five daring missions... five awesome machines! Draw lines to connect each task to the best vehicle for the job.

MISSION A

The Hood has sabotaged air-traffic control. Hundreds of planes are now circling the skies unable to land! This mission needs a high-tech system to communicate with all the pilots and guide the planes down to safety. Who to call?

THUNDERBIRD 2

MISSION B

An old tanker is leaking toxic waste, close to the beautiful Belize Barrier Reef. A craft is needed to reach the seabed, patch up the tanker and safely dispose of the toxic waste. Which vehicle is up to it?

MISSION C

In the Himalayan mountain range, a huge avalanche traps a team of scientists in their lab. This mission could do with some heavy lifting! Can you think of a craft strong enough to pull this off?

THUNDERBIRD 1

THUNDERBIRD 5

THUNDERBIRD 3

MISSION D

High above Earth, a satellite has malfunctioned, throwing GPS signals into chaos. There's global gridlock. The mission requires a craft to fly up to the satellite to perform urgent repairs — which one is most suitable?

MISSION E

A window-cleaning machine on a skyscraper has been hit by lightning. Broken parts are crashing to the ground. A vehicle is needed to quickly travel hundreds of kilometres and recover the machine. Who should go?

THUNDERBIRD 4

ANSWERS ON PAGE 61

MASTER OF DISGUISE

International Rescue find that the number of accidents they are called to is increasing. A mysterious international criminal called 'The Hood' wants to control technology across the world and poses a threat to the Tracy brothers' quests to help others.

THE HOOD

- A master of disguise.
- Can change his appearance in the blink of an eye using a futuristic hologram and nanoscopic light emitters.
- Wants to steal and use cutting-edge technology, including the Thunderbirds vehicles.
- Knows secrets unknown to the Tracy brothers.

LOCATION

His secret base of operation is mobile and modular, allowing The Hood to be based anywhere in the world.

THE HOOD WILL DO JUST ABOUT ANYTHING TO GET HIS HANDS ON THE THUNDERBIRD VEHICLES.

AWESOME ALLIES

International Rescue isn't just about the Tracys. The brothers are supported by a talented team behind the scenes and in the line of fire. Without their help... Thunderbirds wouldn't go!

BRAINS

Intelligent inventor Brains is responsible for designing and building all of the Thunderbird vehicles and tech. He can usually be found in his underground lab on Tracy Island. However, he sometimes goes on missions with the Tracy brothers if they need his expert help.

Nothing's impossible with science!

F.A.B. FACT
Brains built his own lab assistant — a robot helper called M.A.X. Only Brains can understand what M.A.X. is saying!

TANUSHA "KAYO" KYRANO

Don't mess with Kayo! She's an expert in kung fu and hand-to-hand combat! Kayo is in charge of International Rescue's security, as well as being the Tracys' self-defence trainer.
She's a skilful pilot and flies the almost undetectable stealth plane, Thunderbird S.

F.A.B. FACT
Kayo gets her nickname from K.O. — short for knock out. As a young child, she often knocked kung fu opponents out cold!

Spoiling your plans is the best part of my job.

LADY PENELOPE

This smart operator leads a dual life! When she's not being photographed at posh parties, her secret role is being International Rescue's behind-the-scenes 'fixer'. Whenever the Tracy brothers need info or materials, they contact Lady Penelope.

F.A.B. FACT

Lady Penelope has a pet pooch called Sherbert — or Bertie for short. He can often sense danger before anyone else.

"This is rather distressing."

PARKER

Ex-soldier Parker once saved the life of Lady Penelope's father, Lord Creighton-Ward. He now works as her loyal driver and bodyguard. Parker has a shady past, which gives him and Lady Penelope access to the criminal underworld!

Right away, m'lady.

F.A.B. FACT

Parker drives the specially adapted luxury limo, FAB1. It's equipped with gadgets such as an oil-slick dispenser and flame throwers!

WHICH TRACY BROTHER ARE YOU?

Take this test to discover which of the five heroic Tracy brothers you are most like.

1 YOUR TEAM LOSES AN IMPORTANT FOOTBALL MATCH. WHAT DO YOU DO AFTER THE GAME?

A Take the blame for the loss. As team captain you should have done more.

B Head home and have some sleep – you're exhausted!

C Put it down to experience – your team is sure to win next time.

D Crack a joke to cheer up your miserable team-mates.

E Go over the game minute-by-minute and come up with a new strategy for your next match.

2 WHICH OF THESE COLOURS DO YOU WEAR MOST?

A Grey   **B** Red   **C** Green

D Yellow   **E** Orange

5 IT'S YOUR BIRTHDAY. WHAT DO YOU DO TO CELEBRATE?

A A family day out, with lots of organized activities.

B Invite your mates round to watch a movie and eat pizza.

C Go bowling with your friends. You're a strike master!

D Throw an enormous fancy-dress party.

E Nothing much – you don't like a big fuss.

4 IF YOU WERE AN ANIMAL, WHICH ONE OF THESE WOULD YOU BE?

A Dog – you're loyal and always eager to please.

B Cat – you're clever, curious and love to nap.

C Elephant – friends say you're strong and dependable.

D Monkey – you love to have fun!

E Owl – you're the quiet, wise and thoughtful type.

3 YOUR SCHOOL IS CLOSED DUE TO FLOODING, CAUSED BY A BROKEN PIPE. HOW DO YOU SPEND YOUR DAY OFF?

A Rush straight to school to find out if you can help mop up.

B Take it easy! It's the perfect chance to go skateboarding and play video games.

C Offer to mend the broken pipe – you're good at fixing things.

D Turn up at school in your flippers and goggles, just for a laugh!

E Organize a team of volunteers to pump out the water and get the school reopened.

6 WHICH OF THESE JOBS WOULD YOU MOST LIKE WHEN YOU'RE GROWN UP?

A Teacher
B Stunt performer
C Firefighter
D Actor
E Computer programmer

7 YOU HAVE A TRICKY PROJECT TO DO FOR SCHOOL. WHAT DO YOU DO?

A Get stuck in straight away, and hand it in early. You hate leaving things to the last minute.
B Ignore it until the day before and then work really hard to get it done on time.
C Pace yourself by doing a little bit each day.
D Make the assignment fun by including a few gags to make your teacher laugh!
E Get all the info you can first, make a detailed plan and get it done on schedule.

8 WHAT ARE YOUR FAVOURITE TYPES OF SPORT?

A Any team sport – as long as you get to pick the side!
B Mountain biking, snowboarding and skateboarding – you like anything extreme!
C Weightlifting, shot put and hammer – you always like to use your strength.
D Watersports such as swimming, diving and sailing.
E The decathlon – you prefer competing solo to team sports and you're a great all-rounder!

HOW DID YOU DO?

SCOTT
MOSTLY As
You're a born leader, like Scott. Bold and fearless, you tackle problems head-on. You always have a plan, and it bothers you when things don't work out like you wanted. You'll make a great Thunderbird 1 pilot!

ALAN
MOSTLY Bs
You're the perfect astronaut, just like Alan! You're happy to chill out, so people may think you're lazy, but if something needs doing in a hurry, you're on it! When you set your mind to something, you always give it 100 per cent.

VIRGIL
MOSTLY Cs
Like Virgil, you're the best pilot for Thunderbird 2. You prefer doing something physical, rather than cooped up in front of a computer screen. You're a loyal friend and if someone has a problem, you're always on hand to help.

GORDON
MOSTLY Ds
You're most like fun-loving Gordon! Ever the practical joker, you love pulling silly pranks and making your friends laugh. You would also be great at patrolling the oceans in an underwater vehicle.

JOHN
MOSTLY Es
Like John, if you're in charge of Thunderbird 5 everything would run smoothly. You're clever, thoughtful and you always have a problem to solve. You can be a little serious sometimes, so try to lighten up!

BADGE OF HONOUR

Up to date with all the Thunderbirds info? Solved all the puzzles? If you have, the Tracy brothers would like to award you this badge. Next time International Rescue require help on a mission, they might come calling on you...

CAUTION iR

ANSWERS

PAGE 12
MISSION LOG

The mission began with a CALL from John. He alerted us to a runaway TRAIN in Japan. Brains told me to reset the power distribution. It was too big a task to take on SOLO, so he came with me.

With Thunderbird 1 on autopilot, I helped Brains get down to the train. It turns out that he's not confident under PRESSURE. Soon we were heading straight for a head-on collision with a huge MOUNTAIN!

Thunderbird 1 responded to my command immediately. CRISIS averted! We still needed to SLOW the train down, and fast. The trouble was the train computer had locked us out.

I tried to use Thunderbird 1 to slow the train. It worked, but my SHIP went shooting off into the distance. John switched the train to a different track, but we had a new PROBLEM. We were heading straight for Unabara City's main terminal.

John realized that it wasn't a computer VIRUS that had locked us out. It was almost like the train was thinking for itself. Alan worked out that the computer wanted to play a GAME! This helped John decide that he needed to distract the computer LONG enough for us to regain control of the train.

PAGE 18
CODE CONFUSION

Calling Scott Tracy. Arrived in Egypt. Traced the Hood to a secret lair under pyramid. Need sensor equipment urgently. Virgil

PAGE 19

START

FINISH

FAST RESPONSE
PAGE 26
PIECE OF THE ACTION!

1. E 2. A 3. F

DELIVERY DILEMMA

TIME	ITEM	PERSON
09:00	Gyroscope	Brains
12:00	Jetpack	Alan
15:00	Torpedo	Gordon

PAGE 27
ALL ABOARD!

A. Sherbert
B. Parker
C. Kayo
D. Alan

PAGE 38
WRONG ROCKET

FACT OR FIB?

1. True 2. False – he enjoys them
3. False – it's Kayo 4. True 5. True

PAGE 39
ROCK RECOVERY

START

FINISH

PAGE 35
ALL ALANS

ALAN appears four times in the grid.

A	L	A	N
L	N	L	A
A	L	A	L
N	A	L	A

ALAN ALERT

PAGE 43
POOCH PRANK

Sherbert is at D4.

PAGE 46
NAME GAME

1. Lady Penelope
2. Scott Tracy
3. Grandma Tracy
4. Virgil Tracy

John Tracy's name is not included.

ALL CHANGE

PAGE 47
SEARCH AND RESCUE

E	S	R	O	H	A	E	S	W	V
D	I	U	R	L	L	E	H	S	G
O	R	I	B	L	A	A	A	N	A
L	E	O	D	M	L	G	R	M	N
P	V	C	R	E	A	A	K	A	E
H	I	T	B	C	O	R	A	L	M
I	D	O	E	D	I	T	I	C	O
N	A	P	N	W	A	V	E	N	N
T	D	U	E	L	T	R	U	T	E
M	A	S	T	A	R	F	I	S	H

Gordon is rescuing Virgil and Grandma.

PAGE 51
COMMS CONUNDRUM

It's line C.

PAGE 54
WE HAVE A SITUATION!

Mission A – Thunderbird 5
Mission B – Thunderbird 4
Mission C – Thunderbird 2
Mission D – Thunderbird 3
Mission E – Thunderbird 1